Original title:
Life's Like a Big Riddle… But With Cake

Copyright © 2025 Creative Arts Management OÜ
All rights reserved.

Author: Penelope Hawthorne
ISBN HARDBACK: 978-1-80566-119-1
ISBN PAPERBACK: 978-1-80566-414-7

The Tantalizing Tease

A slice so sweet, it calls my name,
With layers stacked, it plays a game.
In every bite, a giggle hides,
A fork in hand, we'll take some rides.

What's hidden deep beneath the glaze?
A flavor dance, a sugary maze.
Crumbs of joy, they tumble down,
In pastry dreams, I wear a crown.

Frosted Facades

The icing swirls in colors bright,
A puppet show of sheer delight.
Behind the frosting, secrets dwell,
With each sweet nibble, stories swell.

A cherry sits, so proud, so round,
But what inside cannot be found?
The cake may frown, or laugh, or sing,
Unraveling joy in every spring.

Savory Secrets

In a pastry box of wonders tall,
A savory riddle amidst it all.
What's that crunch? A joyful cheer,
Is it cheese or a fun-filled smear?

Behind the crust, a mystery lies,
Unexpected flavors in disguise.
A slice of whimsy, a hearty joke,
With every forkful, we stoke the smoke.

Baked Dreams

In the oven, wishes rise,
Transforming dough into surprise.
A sprinkle here, a dash of cheer,
Creating smiles from ear to ear.

With buttered hopes, we take a chance,
A frosted fate, a merry dance.
So grab a piece, let laughter reign,
In every crumb, we taste the gain.

Sweets to Solve

In the oven, secrets rise,
Frosting hides the clever lies.
Every layer tells a tale,
Digging deep, we'll never fail.

Whisk of cream and crumbs do dance,
With each bite, we take a chance.
Sprinkles twinkle like a star,
In this puzzle, sweetly bizarre.

Baked Phantoms

Ghostly treats in shadows creep,
Whispers of the frosting sweep.
Cookies grin with cheeky glee,
   Baking's full of mystery.

Muffins lurking, soft and warm,
Hide the tricks, but hold the charm.
Cupcake towers, tall and bright,
   Portals to a sugary night.

Essence of Enigma

The batter stirs with wit and flair,
Hints of laughter fill the air.
Every bite, a curious quest,
Finding joy in every jest.

Pies and pastries greet the day,
In this conundrum, come what may.
Crusts and fillings hide their thoughts,
What they tell, it can't be bought.

The Sifted Story

Flour dust like secrets fly,
As we bake, let worries die.
Chocolate chips like puzzling clues,
What to choose? We can't lose!

Mixing joy with every scoop,
In this sweet and silly loop.
Jokes abound with every cake,
What we create? A tasty wake.

Delighting in the Unknown

A puzzle baked in layers bright,
With sprinkles of joy, a tasty bite.
Questions swirl like whipped cream clouds,
Each slice a giggle, laughter loud.

What mystery lies within this cake?
Is it a fortune or a mistake?
Maybe frosting hides the truth,
Or a cherry tomfoolery of youth.

Crusts and Queries

Crusts so flaky, secrets to keep,
Behind the glaze, where answers sleep.
Come take a fork and join the fun,
Unravel tales as warm as the sun.

Filled with fruit, or maybe regret,
Every bite's a riddle, don't fret.
The crumbs may whisper, the icing tease,
What tastes the best? Just grab and seize.

Frosting of Fate

Fate's a cupcake with a twist so sweet,
Layered surprises in every treat.
A cherry on top, or is it fate?
Take a big bite, let's celebrate!

Do you dare choose one over the rest?
Each flavor's a chance, a little quest.
Dare to choose chocolate, or berry delight?
Each frosting layer brings sheer delight!

A Carousel of Confections

Round and round, the sweets do spin,
With every turn, a grin to win.
Cotton candy clouds and waffle hills,
A carousel where laughter spills.

What flavor mayhem awaits us next?
A mystery of tastes, oh, how perplexed!
Gumdrops and giggles ignite our pace,
In this sweet ride and funny race.

A Delicate Balance

In the kitchen, we laugh and play,
Flour flies in a sweet ballet.
Eggs crack open, sugar spills,
Mixing joy with a dash of thrills.

Buttercream smiles, spread with flair,
Frosting battles, oh, what a dare!
Layered secrets stacked so high,
Each bite's a mystery, oh my, oh my!

Intricate Icing

Patterns twist in colors bright,
A swirl of mischief, pure delight.
Oh, the sprinkles that dance and cheer,
Each bite whispers, 'Have no fear!'

Candies melt like dreams of yore,
Taste the fun, come back for more.
With every slice, we scratch our heads,
What's the riddle? Who needs meds?

Sugary Surprises

Open the box, what will you find?
Sugary wonders, oh, so kind.
Chocolate puddles and fruity zest,
Guess the flavors, it's a quest!

Biting through the layers divine,
Unexpected flavors intertwine.
A tart lemon hides with glee,
Confusion served with a side of tea!

Dessert of Discovery

With each fork, a riddle awaits,
A journey through sweet, twisty gates.
Meringue clouds and brownie storms,
In this realm, the wacky warms.

So cheer for delight, spread the cheer,
In this dessert, there's nothing to fear.
Slice it, share it, laugh with friends,
The fun in baking never ends!

Sprinkles of Serendipity

In a world of flour and sweet demand,
We mix our dreams with a steady hand.
A dash of chaos, a whimsy swish,
Who knew icing could grant a wish?

Forks in the road and a frosting tide,
With every bite, a new joy to bide.
Chocolate rivers and rainbow paths,
Laughter erupts when we taste the laughs.

Cookies crumbling, that's how it goes,
Each bite taken, a riddle bestows.
But oh, the giggles, they never cease,
For in our kitchens, we find our peace.

So sprinkle the fun and don't be shy,
Whip up a storm, let worries fly.
In every layer, a mystery lies,
Just grab a fork and dig for the prize!

Baking the Unknown

Whisking thoughts in a bowl so bright,
What's next, you ask? A delightful bite!
Mixing flavors that twist and turn,
Each tasted recipe gives us more to learn.

Sifting doubts like powdered sugar,
Laughter bubbles as flavors conjure.
What's hidden deep in the batter holds,
A giggle or two worth more than gold.

Rolling pins and silly fights,
A half-baked joke makes for great delights.
With sprinkles for wishes, we bake and laugh,
Life may puzzle, but we found our path.

From oven's glow to icing's grace,
We dance around at a frosted pace.
So let's embrace the gooey fun,
The dessert of life has just begun!

Sweet Solutions to Bitter Questions

When questions rise like dough on cue,
We search for answers, sweet and true.
With icing pens and a quirky spatula,
Life's mysteries solved with a cupcakeula!

For every query that sinks like lead,
Sprinkles for stress and chocolate spread.
Don't fret too much, don your apron,
In this kitchen, the fun's never flown.

Baking brings clarity, so let's explore,
Each floury problem just opens a door.
So mix those doubts and taste the joke,
In the oven's warmth, all worries choke.

Sugar and spice, a quirky blend,
With every bite, sweet answers send.
We may not know what life will bake,
But for questions asked, there's always cake!

Decoding the Delights of Being

In every crumb, a story unfolds,
The tales of kitchens and laughter told.
A mix of chaos, a dash of charm,
Each slice reveals what keeps us calm.

With cupcakes singing and cookies that dance,
A sprinkle of magic gives life a chance.
From buttercream clouds to jello dreams,
We decode the world in sugary themes.

Layer by layer, we find our way,
Amidst the sweetness, we laugh and play.
So take your fork, dig in, don't wait,
The riddle is answered; it's time to celebrate!

Embrace each flavor, don't hesitate,
In this realm of sweets, it's never late.
So let's bake together, a joyful scheme,
In the kitchen of fun, we find our dream.

The Flavorful Quest

In a kitchen bright and wide,
Mysteries of sweets abide.
Flavors dance in a wild spree,
Chasing dreams as sweet as can be.

Frosting mountains, sugary streams,
Bakers crafting gooey dreams.
With each bite, a giggle spurs,
Taste the joy that always blurs.

Sprinkles splash like laughter's song,
Creating chaos all day long.
In this banquet, we delight,
Finding fun in every bite.

Culinary Curiosities

A donut hole, a secret prize,
With chocolate glaze, oh what a surprise!
Cupcakes whisper tales at noon,
While brownies giggle, 'Let's make a tune!'

Each oven's laugh, a quirky sizzle,
As muffins bop, a playful drizzle.
Cooking's like a treasure hunt,
Find the giggles, play the stunt!

Cookies crumble, tales they weave,
In the batter, dreams believe.
Life's oddities frosted with cheer,
In every kitchen, fun is here!

Whimsical Whiskers

In the whisk's twirl, mischief brews,
Flour fights with playful hues.
A spatula smiles, dancing around,
As the mixer hums a joyous sound.

Peeking spoons with a friendly glare,
Making doughnuts with cheeky flair.
Flavors flirt, oh what a scene,
As sugar sprinkles, sweet and keen!

Pastries prance in silly pairs,
While cupcakes gossip about their wares.
With every bake, a chuckle found,
In this kitchen, laughter's crowned!

Pastry Promises

Tarts that wink and pies that grin,
Each flaky crust a joyful spin.
With jammy treasures tucked inside,
Eating pastries, oh what a ride!

Scones that sing and cookies cheer,
Whisking worries far from here.
Chocolate rivers flow with glee,
In our hearts, the fun runs free!

Every layer hides a jest,
Sweet surprises are the best.
So grab a fork, let laughter soar,
In this baking land, we want more!

Baked Brilliance

In a world of frosting bright,
We laugh at sprinkles in the light.
A slice of pie, a giggle here,
With every fork, we shed a tear.

Each cake reveals a secret treat,
A cherry on the truth so sweet.
We ponder frosting, layers deep,
While cake crumbs dance like dreams from sleep.

The oven hums a playful tune,
As whiskers wiggle by the moon.
With every whisk, a mystery,
And every bite a history.

So gather 'round this tasty feast,
Where laughter grows, and worries cease.
In every slice, a riddle plays,
And in each nibble, joy betrays.

Whims of Whip

Whipped cream clouds float high and wide,
As we indulge, it's quite the ride.
With every dollop, humor flows,
In bursts of laughter, joy just grows.

A pie spins stories of delight,
Each fork a quest, each crumb a flight.
Mother's recipe, a treasure map,
Where guffaws echo in a flap.

Nestled within the cake's soft heart,
We find the quirks that set apart.
A sprinkle here, a giggle there,
In this sweet chaos, none a care.

So whip it good, and let it swirl,
With every twist, let laughter curl.
In kitchens bright with joy so sweet,
We chase the whimsy, not defeat.

The Tasting of Truth

A cupcake whispers secrets bold,
As frosting tales in colors told.
Each bite, a puzzle to untwist,
What flavors hide beneath the mist?

So crumble after crumble break,
The truths that spark with every cake.
Each cherry placed, a question waits,
With answered bites, it never hesitates.

In layers deep, discoveries hide,
Banana jokes that we abide.
A pie's enigma wants to play,
As laughter lingers, come what may.

With fork in hand and heart so bright,
We'll nibble on this sheer delight.
The tasting game is fun, you see,
As sweetness rises, wild and free.

Puzzles in Pastry

Pastry puzzles, secrets sweet,
With every layer, joy we greet.
A flaky crust, a mystery spun,
As crumbs and giggles come undone.

Inside the tart, a riddle waits,
Packed with laughter on our plates.
What flavor hides beneath the glaze?
With forks in hand, we start the craze.

Beneath the icing, chaos reigns,
Flavors burst, and no one gains.
We ponder what the next slice shares,
And giggle madly, none of us cares.

So slice it up, let's dive right in,
Where pastry fun and giggles begin.
In every crumble, joy resides,
With riddles wrapped in sweet delights.

A Recipe for Discovery

In the kitchen of dreams, we bake,
Flours of laughter mixed with a shake.
Sugar-coated moments rise and swell,
Each slice a journey, oh what a spell!

Eggs of curiosity crack with glee,
Batter of questions, just let it be.
Ovens of chaos, we twirl and spin,
The frosting of joy waits patiently within.

The Secret Ingredient

A dash of chaos, a pinch of fun,
Sprinkled gold dust when day is done.
Measure your woes, and mix them right,
Find sweetness hidden, even in fright.

A secret blend, not found in books,
It's laughter's spice and honeyed looks.
Bake your troubles, let them rise high,
With every layer, watch spirits fly!

Whipped Whispers

In a bowl of dreams, we whisk away,
Whipped whispers of joy in a sunny play.
Fold in treasures and sprinkle in glee,
With every swirl, set your heart free.

Laughter's lightness, so fluffy and bright,
Every blend shares its own silly bite.
Layers of giggles and icing so thick,
Funny little tales, that's our magic trick!

Slices of Solitude

In a corner stands a cake all alone,
Slices of solitude, a funny tone.
Each forkful taken, a truth revealed,
Beneath the frosting, the heart's concealed.

So take a piece and don't feel shy,
With every nibble, let laughter fly.
In the silence, flavors dance and play,
A silent party, hip-hip-hooray!

Icing on the Unanswered Questions

In every slice, a mystery brews,
Frosted thoughts, with sparks and clues.
Baking dreams with laughter and sprinkles,
Hiding answers in chocolate crinkles.

Where do missing socks always go?
Is it the icing or just the dough?
With crumbs of wisdom in each bite,
We chew on questions, day and night.

Cupboards creak with secrets untold,
Sifting through laughter, daring and bold.
A pie chart of smiles, none left to waste,
Savoring riddles with every taste.

Uneven Slices of Truth

Life's a cake, but who gets the pie?
Unequal portions make us ask why.
Layered lies and sweet candor blend,
Grabbing forks, we just want to mend.

The surprises in layers, like life's ups and downs,
We slice through the sweetness, wearing our crowns.
A dash of confusion, a sprinkle of cheer,
In this bakery of truth, hold your dear.

Ganache of Grief and Joy

Two flavors swirl in each little bite,
Bitter and sweet, a delightful sight.
Filling our lives with both laughter and tears,
Ganache of moments fills all our years.

Whisk it together, don't let it curdle,
In the oven of time, there's always a hurdle.
Joyful frosting can cover a bruise,
With a side of acceptance, there's nothing to lose.

The Puzzle Pâtissier

Baking up riddles with flour and fun,
The puzzle pâtissier never did run.
Layering flavors, a dash of delight,
Tasting the chaos, both wrong and right.

With a sprinkle of patience and a pinch of wit,
Every odd bake makes the whole thing a hit.
The oven hums with secrets and cheer,
As laughter rises, we draw ever near.

Crumble the Code

In the kitchen, flour flies,
Mixing secrets with sweet surprise.
Eggs and sugar, a playful blend,
Solving puzzles, on treats we depend.

Frosting techniques, oh what a mess,
Each layer stacked, it's anyone's guess.
The oven buzzes, a riddle unfolds,
It's a game of taste, or so I'm told.

With sprinkles scattered, we take a bite,
Unraveling flavors, a delightful flight.
Crumbs of laughter dance through the air,
In this bake-off, there's joy everywhere.

So grab your mixer, don't be shy,
Let's whisk away worries, oh my oh my!
Each slice we cut, brings giggles and cheer,
In this world of treats, we've nothing to fear.

The Whipped Whimsy

A dollop of cream, a dash of fun,
Whip it good, we've only begun.
Sprinkling dreams with a cherry on top,
In our pastry world, we'll never stop.

Mixing colors, a rainbow delight,
Each bite a giggle, a sugary sight.
The taste buds tango, oh, what a show,
With every forkful, our smiles do grow.

A banter of flavors, frosted and sweet,
Chasing our woes with sugary beats.
Laughter erupts with each playful taste,
Creating memories, no time to waste.

So come, my friend, join in this spree,
Let's bake a puzzle, just you and me.
With frosting and fun, our worries will flee,
In this whipped wonder, we're truly free!

Foundations of Flavor

With every layer, a story to tell,
Of sweet adventures, oh can't you tell?
Baking logic, a recipe's tease,
Filling our plates with flavors to please.

Flour detective in search of a clue,
What works best, lemon or goo?
Mix in the giggles, frosting galore,
Here's to surprises—let's bake some more!

Crusts and crumbles, a delightful base,
In this kitchen, there's no such race.
With spatulas ready, we laugh and we play,
Building our dreams in a most tasty way.

So gather 'round friends, let's have a slice,
Decoding desserts, isn't it nice?
In the depths of the oven, our joy will arise,
With each crumbly wonder, there's laughter in pies.

Candied Clues

A sprinkle of mystery, a dash of delight,
Each sugary moment feels just right.
Gumball puzzles, candies to chase,
In this sweet game, we quicken our pace.

Dip in the chocolate, swirl it around,
In each sticky situation, joy can be found.
Caramel trails lead us astray,
Laughter erupts as we play and sway.

Marzipan questions and frosting replies,
Unwrapping joy in a clever disguise.
As crumbs gather round, adventures will bloom,
In our candy-coated world, there's always room.

So let's share the laughter, the sweet and the fun,
With candy and cake, our hearts weigh a ton.
Discovering secrets in each tasty bite,
In this riddle of flavors, everything feels right.

Deliciously Confounded Journeys

In a world where frosting swirls,
Questions dance like playful girls.
With sprinkles scattered far and wide,
Who knew joy could be our guide?

The crumbs hold secrets, sweet and neat,
As I ponder each tasty treat.
A slice of pie, a puzzling bite,
What's the answer? Oh, what a fright!

Grocery aisles are curious mazes,
I search for clues in chocolate blazes.
The pastries whisper tales untold,
In every nibble, pure delight unfolds.

So grab a fork, join in the fun,
For every riddle burns like the sun.
With cakes and pies, we'll never fret,
The journey's sweet; don't place your bet!

Conundrums in Confection

Cupcakes giggle, muffins tease,
What's the mystery in this cheese?
Baker with flour dusted on cheeks,
What's the secret? I must sneak peaks!

Filling layers with creamy dreams,
Even whipped icing has its schemes.
Try to solve the tart's great show,
Will the frosting guide, or overflow?

Pies and cookies hold their breath,
In the kitchen, we flirt with death.
Oh, the batter splatters wide,
Caught in riddles, we cannot hide!

Take a bite, let the fun commence,
Every nibble raises suspense.
Chocolate chips, a playful clue,
In every dessert, life's tasty brew!

Sugar-Coated Mysteries

In the pantry, sweet surprises,
Jelly beans hold subtle disguises.
The caramel's voice, rich and low,
Leads me where I do not know.

Sifting flour reveals odd truths,
Buttercream whispers, sharing flutes.
A slice of wonder, a dash of luck,
In this dessert, I'm happily stuck!

Whimsical whisks and merry jars,
Count the sprinkles, count the stars.
Chocolate fountains can't be tamed,
Will any question stay unnamed?

With gummy bears as my allies,
Together we'll reach for the skies.
So laugh and crunch through every layer,
For secrets hide in every flavor!

Tiers of Complexity

A tower of goodies, stacked so high,
With frosting clouds that almost fly.
What's the riddle beneath each bite?
Piecing together the wrongs and rights.

Syrup streams like laughter, bold,
Every layer, a story told.
Yet among the bites of gooey bliss,
Lies the question I cannot miss.

Frosted enigmas filled with cream,
Life, it seems, is but a dream.
Count the layers, lose the track,
What awaits if I bite back?

So dig in deep, don't spare the fork,
With each discovery, we can gawk.
The sweetness swirls, so come and take,
In every riddle, there's joy to make!

The Cake Chronicles

Each slice tells a story, oh so sweet,
With frosting like laughter, a sugary treat.
Baking mishaps become part of the fun,
Where every mistake is a chance to run!

Eggs in a scramble, flour on my face,
A recipe's chaos, a whimsical race.
Candles like wishes, they flicker and sway,
Making my troubles all melt away.

A mix of despair, a dash of delight,
Whipping up joy in the kitchen tonight.
As layers stack high, I giggle and cheer,
With each little bite, I'll conquer my fear.

So here's to the layers, both thick and thin,
In this riddle of baking, let the fun begin!
For in every cupcake, there's wisdom to find,
A slice of happy, for heart and for mind.

Layers of Meaning

Beneath the icing, secrets do hide,
Like feelings and flavors that swirl inside.
Some days are butter, while others are jam,
A whimsical puzzle, oh what a plan!

Flour sifts gently, like dreams as they rise,
Baking's a journey, a fun little surprise.
Eggshells crack open to let laughter in,
Who knew this riddle would start with a grin?

A sprinkle of joy, a dash of despair,
With every sweet layer, come giggles to share.
Chocolate and cherry, a delightful mess,
Finding the meaning, I must confess.

With forks in our hands, we tackle this cake,
Each bite a riddle, a twist I must take.
So let's feast together, in this sugary land,
For in every cake slice, love's waiting, unplanned.

Toppled Tiers

Three layers of laughter, stacked high and wide,
But oh, what a showdown when they collide!
A toppled creation, a frosting surprise,
The faces around me are wide-eyed with sighs.

It tumbled and rolled, a chaotic delight,
A cake catastrophe turned festive tonight.
With sprinkles a-flying, we burst into fits,
Who knew a mishap could lead to such hits?

The candles are wobbling, the platter's a mess,
Yet giggles erupt, oh, what a success!
Beneath all the frosting, we savor the bliss,
In the wreckage of layers, we find pure happiness.

So we gather the crumbs, with smiles on our faces,
In the wreck of a cake, we found our embraces.
For laughter's the icing when things go awry,
With memories baked in, we reach for the sky.

Secrets in the Batter

In bowls full of secrets, I stir and I blend,
With giggles and whispers, my trusty friend.
A pinch of confusion, a splash of the fun,
The mystery thickens, the baking's begun.

Eggs crack with laughter, oh what a sound,
As sugar and chaos whirl joyfully 'round.
Each layer I foster, each texture I seek,
A puzzle unfolds, unique with each week.

Vanilla or chocolate, old recipes tease,
Whisking my worries like leaves in the breeze.
For every misstep leads to a grin,
A cakey adventure, let's dive right in!

So gather your friends, let the whisking commence,
With secrets and giggles, we'll bake with a sense.
In every sweet bite, there's a riddle to face,
With laughter as frosting, we cherish this space.

A Confectioner's Quest for Clarity

In the pantry of my mind, I search for crumbs,
Frothy thoughts like whipped cream, they dance and hum.

Sugar-coated questions swirl in the air,
Buttercream answers, can I find a pair?

With every sprinkle, I chase the muse,
Chocolate chips of wisdom, I get to choose.
Baking my plans like a frosted delight,
Hoping the oven warms up my insight.

Laughter is the whisk that stirs my bowl,
Oops! A little eggshell, that's just the role.
Mixing and folding, a delicious feat,
Confectioner's dilemma, I'm feeling sweet!

So here I stand, apron covered in flour,
Searching for reason in the baking hour.
With each slice I take from the pie of dreams,
I ponder the puzzle, or so it seems.

The Bake Shop of Thoughts

Welcome to the shop where ideas rise,
Buns of brilliance, oh what a surprise!
Cupcakes of chaos swirl on the shelf,
I taste a few, then come back for myself.

Sifting through moments, like flour in the air,
Whisking away troubles with creamy flair.
Jars filled with giggles line all the walls,
Pastries of laughter, where joy never stalls.

Mixing my worries in batter so bold,
Each pinch of humor, a treasure to hold.
Baking new thoughts until golden brown,
What's the next flavor? Let's not wear a frown!

From muffins of madness to pies of delight,
I craft my concoctions to balance the fright.
In this bakery realm, there's no fear nor shame,
Just sugar and sprinkles in a whimsical game.

Layered Dilemmas and Sweet Resolutions

In layers of frosting, dilemmas arise,
Each slice reveals secrets, oh what a surprise!
Caramel chaos with a dash of cool,
Digging for answers in my sweet baking tool.

Weighing the options like flour in a bowl,
Tossed with decision like sprinkles on a roll.
Riddles of icing, a puzzle to taste,
Each forkful a chapter, not a crumb to waste.

Marzipan mountains and raspberry streams,
Bite-sized solutions hide in my dreams.
With every layer, I rise to the quest,
Finding sweet endings is surely the best!

So here's to the journey, each flavor we try,
Mixing up moments like pastry in pie.
Through sticky dilemmas and creamy delight,
We bake up our laughter, it feels just right.

The Cakewalk Through Chaos

In a world of sprinkles, I dance and sway,
Cakewalk through chaos, I giggle and play.
Frosted conundrums swirl all around,
Bouncing on batter where joy can be found.

Whipped up confusions and marzipan cheer,
Every wild moment is perfectly clear.
Slicing through mayhem with humor and grace,
Taste-testing troubles, oh what a chase!

With a dash of mischief and frosting so bright,
I twirl through the kitchen, feeling just right.
Confetti and laughter, they fill up the space,
Building sweet memories in this baking race.

So come grab a slice of this jolly parade,
In my bake-off world, there's no need to fade.
Together we'll sprinkle and savor the night,
As we cakewalk through chaos, everything's light!

The Flavor of Life

In a world of frosting, sweet and bright,
We ponder flavors, day and night.
A sprinkle of joy, a dash of doubt,
What's the cake about?

With layers of laughter, cream so thick,
Slice it up quick, don't miss a trick.
Each bite a question, each bite a joke,
Watch as the mystery provokes.

We add some cherries, a twist of fate,
Is it too early, or perhaps too late?
Each crumb we gather tells a tale,
In this bakery of life, we cannot fail.

Baking together, we rise and fall,
What was the secret? We can't recall.
With icing on dreams, we laugh and play,
What flavor is this, anyway?

Whipping Up Questions

Stirring the pot, oh what a blend,
Is it sugar, is it spice, or a trend?
A pinch of chaos, a spoonful of fate,
What's your recipe to elevate?

Mixing and mashing, here comes the mess,
Life's a question, we guess and guess.
Rolling in laughter, we rise to the top,
Can we figure it out? Nope, never will stop!

Eggs cracking open, surprises inside,
With each whiff, we giggle and slide.
Bake it with love, take a chance,
What is the answer in this baking dance?

Whipping up questions like cream on a pie,
Are we experts, or just asking why?
In the kitchen of life, let's make a mess,
It's all part of this fun, we confess.

A Slice of Serendipity

Caught in a moment, just like a cake,
Sweet surprises make our sides ache.
A slice of luck, a nibble of fate,
What's this dish? Can you relate?

Frosted dreams with a cherry on top,
Will we savor it, or let it flop?
Dancing through layers, we stumble and swirl,
In this banquet of life, it's all a whirl!

A surprise in every mouthful we share,
Finding delight in the crumbs everywhere.
A riddle of flavors, a puzzle to pick,
What's the answer? Just take a lick!

Sprinkled with joy, served warm on a plate,
Timing is everything, or could it be fate?
Savor each moment, don't let them flit,
In this crazy bake-off, we're all a bit lit!

Garnished with Mystery

A dusting of powder, what's under that?
Tastes like a riddle, odd as a cat.
Decorated dreams, but what's inside?
Too many flavors make us divide.

Filling with humor, a layer of wack,
Is that chocolate or a crooked quack?
The cake looks perfect, but wait—what's this?
A hidden fruit that we might miss!

Slice through the chaos, see what you find,
The essence of wonder, forever aligned.
Garnished with laughter, a twist on the fork,
The riddle is tasty, let's not just talk!

Scoop it together, let's make a plate,
Every bite's a mystery to contemplate.
With a wink and a smile, enjoy the parade,
In this cake of confusion, let's never fade.

Craving the Clue

In the kitchen, flour flies high,
Baking secrets, oh my, oh my!
I mix and stir, what will I find?
A twist of fate, a taste of blind.

The oven's warm, a curious heat,
Is it a cake or something sweet?
I take a guess, mix up a dream,
A slice of laughter, or so it seems.

Frosting swirls, a rainbow parade,
In frosting trails, my worries fade.
Every bite's a puzzle piece,
In this cake quest, I find my peace.

With sprinkles dancing, I ponder still,
What's the answer? Do I have skill?
A cake, a riddle, both quite absurd,
In this sweet chaos, joy's not inferred!

Cakes of Curiosity

A tower of layers, stacked up high,
Each tier a riddle, oh me, oh my!
Chocolate whispers, vanilla sighs,
In every bite, a sweet surprise.

With forks in hand, we take our chance,
To savor sweetness, join the dance.
What's hiding here? A secret treat,
In creamy dreams, we taste the beat.

Is it lemon zesty or berry bright?
Each crumb confounds, yet feels so right.
We gather 'round, with laughter clear,
In this cake conundrum, joy draws near.

An icing swirl, a playful game,
With every morsel, we stake our claim.
To live in riddles, sweet and fine,
In cakes of wonder, we always dine!

Sweet Solutions

Beneath the icing, mysteries hide,
Flavors collide like a wild ride.
I slice a piece, dive into the fun,
What secret lies beneath, or is it just a pun?

A cherry on top, a jiggly jig,
With every bite, I dance a big gig.
What's the answer? Oh, who can tell?
In this sugary maze, all is well.

Frosted puzzles, sprinkled cheer,
What's the solution hiding here?
Each cake a riddle, each bite so sly,
There's sweet wisdom in layers piled high.

In tasty bites, we chase delight,
Unraveling puzzles, in moonlit night.
With crumbs of laughter, we bake our fate,
In the humor of sweetness, we celebrate.

Sugar-Coated Mysteries

A cake stands tall, with secrets dressed,
In sugar-coated layers, oh, I'm blessed!
What flavors swirl beneath the glaze?
In this confection, I lose my gaze.

Every slice reveals a tale,
Chocolate whispers, strawberry gale.
We laugh and wonder, share the thrill,
What's next to taste? It's a baker's will.

Sprinkles twinkle, frosting charms,
In our foodie quest, we guard our arms.
Like a detective, I take a spoon,
Unearthing laughter, morning to noon.

With forks like probes, we dig away,
In this cake treasure, we laugh and play.
A sugary riddle, in bites so grand,
Together we feast, with joy unplanned!

Cake as Metaphor

A sprinkle of joy, a dash of fright,
Layers of dreams stacked up so high.
Frosting the truth with sweet delight,
Each bite we take, we wonder why.

Crumbs of wisdom fall to the floor,
Glimpses of mystery taste like bliss.
Baking up questions we can't ignore,
Who knew dessert could lead to this?

The oven's hot, the timer beeps,
A layer of laughs, a pinch of fate.
With every slice, a secret seeps,
Let's serve confusion on a plate!

In every corner, a riddle hides,
With chocolate chips to guide the way.
We eat and ponder, our cake abides,
Who knew the fun could flavor the day?

The Recipe for Revelation

A cup of hope, a spoon of jest,
Mix them well, watch laughter rise.
Bake for hours, let humor rest,
A slice revealed, a sweet surprise.

Ingredients blend in chaotic dance,
Whisking thoughts, stirring delight.
Every layer a whimsical chance,
To savor wisdom in every bite.

Pouring doubts like batter anew,
Sprinkle in tales both weird and wacky.
Just when you think you've cracked the view,
The cake erupts, oh so tacky!

Slice by slice, the laughter grows,
With frosting thick on every thought.
In every piece, a new one shows,
To reveal what life's really bought!

The Joy of Discovery

In the oven, an adventure brews,
Mysteries rise with heat and glee.
What flavor lies behind those hues?
Is it vanilla? Is it mystery?

A frosted grin, a flaky cheer,
Each bite a quest, a puzzle to solve.
With every morsel, we shed our fear,
And watch the world slowly evolve.

Cakes of laughter, crumbles of fun,
Slicing through the frosting, we find,
Every layer a journey begun,
With icing that tickles the mind.

So here's to the flavors yet to see,
In this kitchen where giggles bake.
Let's devour the joy and simply be,
As we laugh through our cake-filled wake!

Cravings and Contemplations

A craving struck, oh what a feat!
Frosting dreams swirl in my head.
Temptations served on a pieced sheet,
Each whim does dance where crumbs have led.

Thoughts mix wild like batter whipped,
What's baked in life, what's yet to mix?
In every slice, a secret tipped,
And in those layers, the truest tricks.

Sprinkles stand like stars up high,
Questions flutter like icing too.
Do we dive in, or just ask why?
The cake calls out, "Come get your view!"

So grab a fork, let's make a mess,
Conversations rise with each new taste.
A slice of wisdom is anyone's guess,
With cake for now, we'll never waste!

The Frosted Puzzle

In every layer, secrets lie,
With sprinkles on top, oh my!
Sugar-coated questions rise,
Who knew baking held such ties?

A cherry here, a candied flair,
Confusion mixed with frosting rare.
Whisking thoughts in a big bowl,
What's the recipe for a whole?

Cherries may drop, and flour may fly,
Yet laughter blends with every pie.
Measurements tease, and counters hum,
What's the scoop? Oh, here we crumb!

Bakers giggle, tarts rejoice,
In the kitchen, we find our voice.
So let's batter up and not delay,
For sweet surprises lead the way!

A Whisk of Wonder

Grab your whisk, it's time to bake,
A pinch of joy, and watch the cake!
Mix the laughter, stir the fun,
With every beat, we come undone!

The oven hums a happy tune,
While frosting dreams burst like a balloon.
A sprinkle here, a giggle there,
Baking chaos fills the air!

Measure the smiles, toss in some glee,
What's the secret recipe?
Each slice reveals another jest,
A yummy riddle, sugar dressed!

Frosted wonders, all aglow,
Baking wit in every row.
Cut the cake, what do we find?
Sweet surprises blow our minds!

Crumbs of Clarity

Under crumbs, the truth is found,
In every bite, a clue is bound.
Chocolate chips and fruity bits,
Bring forth laughter, never quits!

Oven mitts, a kitchen race,
Flour dust paints a silly face.
Find the humor in the mess,
With every taste, we are blessed!

Dough may rise, but so do we,
Bouncing joy, so carefree.
Slicing hints with every share,
Cake makes riddles all laid bare!

From ganache drips, we take a peek,
In every layer, a giggling streak.
Life's sweet layers, catch your breath,
With every bite, we cheat our death!

Slice Through the Mystery

With each slice, a puzzle solved,
In frosting dreams, our fate evolved.
Surprises hide in fluffy cream,
What could it be? Just take a beam!

Cherry glaze and lemon zest,
Crack the code, it's for the best.
Layer by layer, taste the fun,
With every fork, we come undone!

Whisk away worry, blend it light,
Ingredients swirling, what a sight!
Laughter echoes, ovens roar,
A scrumptious riddle we explore!

So here's a toast to cakes and cheer,
To every crumby truth we hear.
So slice and share, don't hesitate,
For with each bite, we celebrate!

The Culinary Enigma

In a kitchen so bright, where the ovens hum,
Mixing flour and sugar, a sugary drum.
Sifting secrets with a pinch of salt,
What's the answer? Only the cake knows, not false!

Eggs crack with glee as they dive right in,
Butter decides it's a playful sin.
A recipe scribbled in a language bizarre,
Yet somehow, dessert is never too far!

Chocolate chips wink like they're part of the game,
Whipping cream giggles, it's never the same.
With a dash of confusion and sprinkles of fun,
The cake pops up, saying, "Hey, I'm done!"

So grab your forks and don't be shy,
For each slice reveals a new piece of pie.
In this puzzling bake-off, we find our delight,
With crumbs of laughter, we'll savor the night!

Frosting the Unknown

Whispers of frosting swirl in the air,
Cakes and conundrums mingle with flair.
Each layer hides tales, sweet and absurd,
In the land of desserts, all mysteries blurred.

Baking soda's giggles rise into the sky,
While vanilla echoes a soft, dreamy sigh.
What comes next? Oh, let's take a guess,
With sprinkles of cheer, we can't help but bless!

A buttercream smile, so witty and wide,
Layers of laughter we just can't abide.
With each frosted secret that slowly unfurls,
We dive into sweetness, a dance of bright swirls!

So join in the party with pie in your hand,
Find bliss in the chaos, it's simply grand.
In this dessert riddle, oh what a show,
Each bite is a giggle, let's all go with the flow!

The Pastry Paradox

Oh, the dough stretches out with a curious flip,
Rolling out mysteries, each one a trip.
Pastries rise up, confounding our brains,
Is it dessert time? Or are we just playing?

A pie in the face of a puzzling plight,
With whipped cream tactics, we giggle with delight.
Who would have thought a muffin could rhyme?
In the oven of chaos, we savor the time!

With a swirl of icing like thoughts in a haze,
Our taste buds are caught in a sugary maze.
While cookies conspire in the warmth of the tray,
They whisper their secrets in a crumbly way.

So slice up the pie with a side of pure fun,
In this paradox of treats, we know we have won.
Bake up the laughter, let sweetness collide,
In this pastry puzzle, joy's always inside!

Candied Reflections

In a mirror of sugar, reflections appear,
Gummy bears dance, spreading laughter and cheer.
With a sprinkle of sugar, we ponder aloud,
What sweet little secrets are hidden in clouds?

Jelly beans tumble like thoughts in a storm,
While caramel swirls take on a new form.
Each bite we devour is filled with surprise,
What riddle awaits? Just look in their eyes!

Chocolate fountains flow like a river of fun,
Who knew a dessert could make us all run?
Cotton candy skies fluff up the chat,
As cupcakes jump in, "Can you handle that?"

So gather around, let's toast with a treat,
On this candied journey, we claim our sweet seat.
In this whirling dilemma, where giggles are fed,
We find joy in the riddle, with sweets in our head!

Mysteries Baked to Perfection

In the oven, secrets swirl,
Frosting dreams begin to twirl.
A sprinkle here, a dash of glee,
What's the answer? Wait and see!

Cakes that wobble, pies that gleam,
Baking triumphs, oh what a dream!
Crumbs of wisdom hide with flair,
Follow the scents, if you dare!

Slices served with a wink and grin,
Each bite's a giggle, let's begin!
Don't ask how, just enjoy the tease,
In this riddle, we bake with ease!

So grab a fork, don't hesitate,
Every layer holds a tasty fate.
With each delicious, gooey slice,
The mystery's sweet, oh what a nice!

The Flavors of the Unsolved

Mystery whisked in bowls of cheer,
Flavorful answers that draw us near.
Lemon twists and chocolate sighs,
Each scrumptious bite, a tasty surprise!

Sifting thoughts like powdered dough,
What's the truth? Only cakes know.
With every layer, secrets blend,
Sweetly served with a twist, my friend.

Pies that puzzle, tarts that tease,
What's the recipe? Can you please?
In every slice, a story told,
A feast of flavors, bright and bold!

So raise a fork, take a chance,
In this banquet, join the dance.
With laughter baked in every cheer,
The answer's here, just grab a beer!

Pies That Defy Explanation

Crusts of wonder, fillings bright,
Confusing talk, but feels so right.
Why does pineapple wear a crown?
In pie form, it won't let us down!

Baked with giggles, frosted dreams,
What's inside? It's not as it seems.
Cherry questions and blueberry lies,
In every forkful, a sweet surprise!

Layers of laughter, zesty delight,
Each slice glowing, oh what a sight!
It's a puzzle that's tasty, no doubt,
Find the flavor, give us a shout!

So let's indulge, don't hold back,
Unearth the mysteries we might lack.
With cream on top and joy for free,
Who knew pies could be such glee?

Frosted Questions and Chewy Answers

Whipped cream clouds, a puzzling delight,
Frosted questions dance in the light.
Why do we bake when the sun is bright?
Cake is the answer, let's take a bite!

Chocolate rivers flow in streams,
Gooey mysteries wrap us in dreams.
Each chewy moment, a laugh unfolds,
In sugary answers, nostalgia holds!

Layers stacked with fluffy glee,
Craving the truth, as sweet as can be.
With cookies crumbling and brownies bold,
Every snack tells a tale to be told!

So lather on sprinkles, no fears to face,
In the realm of desserts, find your place.
With frosting dripping and smiles that grow,
The truth's in the cake; let's bake and glow!

Savory Secrets of Existence

Peeking through layers, bright and sweet,
A conundrum waits with every treat.
Whisking the answers, flour on my nose,
I bake my questions, where curiosity grows.

Mixing a batter of joy and despair,
A sprinkle of hope hangs in the air.
Stirring frustrations like eggs in a bowl,
With each fold I find a deeper goal.

Hints in the frosting, shapes out of place,
With icing as clues, I'm saving my face.
A slice of the mystery, bite at a time,
The secret's not bitter, just playful and sublime.

Rolling through life with a fondant so sweet,
The questions arise as I mix up the heat.
Yeast of existence, rising with pride,
In this kitchen of chaos, I joyfully hide.

Sugar and Spice in Life's Puzzle.

Doughy dilemmas, rolling on the table,
Trying to solve them as best as I'm able.
Sprinkles of laughter, crumbs of the past,
Each slice of the puzzle, so fun to outlast.

A pinch of confusion, a dollop of cheer,
Baking my way through what I hold dear.
Flavorful questions, garnished in glee,
The answers are sweeter when shared with tea.

Frosting my worries, turning them bright,
Add a cherry on top, it's a beautiful sight.
With giggles and chuckles, I mix and I knead,
In this zany oven, I follow my creed.

Mixing the flavors, as odd as they sound,
The cake holds the secrets that swirl all around.
In each tasty layer, a riddle does dwell,
I slice through the laughter, I'm under its spell.

Layers of Enigmas

In a pie dish of questioning, crumbles abound,
Slicing through riddles that spin round and round.
Each flaky layer, a mystery unfolds,
Sticky with secrets that never grow old.

With each spoonful of nonsense, I chew on my thoughts,
Searching for answers but finding more knots.
A dash of confusion, a swirl of surprise,
Tasting the truths with wide-open eyes.

Whipping up wonders in this curious mix,
I find the key to these puzzling tricks.
The cake of existence, both sweet and absurd,
Crumbs of the quandary are all that I've stirred.

Layer by layer, I search for the clue,
In the chocolatey chaos, I find the best brew.
Each bite brings a giggle, a sigh, or a cheer,
Cooking up riddles with sprinkles of cheer.

Sweet Confusion

A cupcake conundrum on a plate so divine,
Frosted with whimsy, a taste quite benign.
In a swirl of confusion, I dig with delight,
The sweetness of life feels perfectly right.

Piping the patterns of questions galore,
Every taste brings new mysteries to explore.
With jellybean jumbles and gummy despair,
I laugh through the layers, flavors in the air.

In a mousse of absurdity, I dare to take flight,
Floating on marshmallows, I'm lost in the white.
Cakes tumble and giggle, the riddles take form,
Crafted in sugar, a playful sweet storm.

So I sip through the challenges, a smooth espresso,
Finding joy in the chaos like it's a grand fresco.
Dessert-making puzzles, oh what a delight,
I savor each moment, wrapped up in the bite.

Flavors of Fate

In the kitchen, chaos reigns,
Frosting spills like runaway trains.
Chocolate dreams and fruit parade,
Sweet disasters, brownies made.

Ovens giggle, yeast takes flight,
Candies dance and sprinkles bite.
Recipes lost, oh what a plight,
Yet taste buds cheer for each delight.

The batter sings a silly tune,
Whipped cream clouds float to the moon.
Every slice holds a secret treat,
With every bite, we can't be beat.

So gather 'round, let laughter bake,
Embrace the mess that every cake makes.
For in this whimsy, smiles will bloom,
Amongst the flour, joy finds room.

Baking the Unknown

A pinch of whimsy, a dash of fun,
Mix it together, see what's spun.
Strange ingredients in a bowl,
Whisking madness till we roll.

The egg just winked, did it smile?
This baking quest is quite the trial.
Sugar's plotting, cinnamon schemes,
In the oven, we chase our dreams.

What's that bubbling? A frothy surprise,
Lemon meringue starts to rise.
Chasing flavors, round we go,
What's it gonna taste like? Who knows, who knows!

Giggling flour, the clock ticks fast,
Baking mysteries, unsurpassed.
With every bite a new affair,
Bring on the laughs, we'll share and share!

A Confectioner's Dilemma

The cake is layered, oh what heights,
But fondant's giving me some frights.
A wobbly tower, sweet and tall,
Will it stay, or will it fall?

Caramel sauce like silly glue,
Dripping down, what will we do?
Chocolate blobs on the kitchen floor,
Where did that frosting go? We need more!

Baker's dozen full of doubt,
Should I add nuts or leave them out?
Taste tests turning into bakeshop wars,
Who knew pure joy would come with chores?

Yet through the chaos, we find the fun,
Biting in, oh what have we done?
A confectioner's heart is wild and free,
For in each mishap, there's joy, you see!

Crusts of Complexity

Crusts are crumbling, edges stray,
As pie charts turn and twist their way.
A recipe's more like an art, you see,
With every slice, a new mystery.

Butter whispers, "Don't overwork,"
While phantom crumbs begin to lurk.
Pastry dreams and doughy fights,
Rolling pins sing through the nights.

What will rise, what will flop?
A nervous breath with every drop.
Pies and tarts in cheeky pose,
With every bake, our laughter grows.

So take a chance on messy crusts,
In baking fun, we ignite our lusts.
For in the end, it's clear as day,
A flaky pie brings glee our way!

Sweet Enigmas of Existence

In the oven hot, truth may rise,
Like a soufflé, hiding its surprise.
Sprinkles of laughter, crumbs of thought,
Deciphering joy is what we've sought.

A slice of joy, a fork in hand,
Whipped cream clouds, oh so grand.
Chocolate rivers, sweet delight,
In this puzzle, we take a bite.

Each bite a question, each taste a clue,
Is frosting the answer, or maybe two?
Happy accidents, oh what a treat,
When flavors swirl, we're in for a feat.

So let's bake on, with giggles and cheer,
In this mysterious cake, we conquer fear.
With every layer, life's quirks we face,
In the end, it's all a sugary race.

Coated Dilemmas and Frosted Dreams

Pies in the sky, secrets so sweet,
Layered dilemmas, what a fun feat!
Sugar-coated laughs, frosting so fine,
Let's ponder the flavors, one bite at a time.

Chocolate chips hide, oh what a jest,
In this confection, we find our quest.
Confusion blends with caramel swirl,
In this tasty world, watch flavors twirl!

Gugelhupf giggles, macaroon charms,
In this tasty quest, who needs alarms?
Pie charts scatter, so tasty and bright,
What flavor's next? A sweetened delight!

So throw out your worries, leave them back there,
Let's sprinkle this moment with fruity flair.
With doughnut dreams and cookie plans,
We dance through riddles, hand in hand.

The Confectioner's Paradox

Cupcakes adorned with riddles galore,
Whipped up questions, who could ask for more?
In every layer, mystery brews,
A puzzling treat, for me and you.

Lollipops whisper secrets unheard,
Sugary tales, oh so absurd!
Each frosting swirl spins a new plot,
What flavor next? I've lost the thought!

Baking and laughing, what a fine mess,
Dessert dilemmas we gladly confess.
With every bite, truth seems to fold,
In layers of laughter, we are consoled.

So let's share our slices, and giggle away,
In this fun conundrum, let's make merry today.
For in every cake, a quip we'll find,
Life's sweetest puzzles, oh, how they bind!

Layers of Whimsy and Wonder

Baked with mischief, each crumb a jest,
Frosted meanings put to the test.
In the kitchen chaos, we frolic and play,
What's up next in our doughy ballet?

Whipped cream allusions tickle the brain,
Serious questions drowned in the rain.
A torte of giggles, a pie of sighs,
With every forkful, the truth slowly flies.

Brownies with barriers, fudge so thick,
Each layer peeled back reveals the trick.
Sugar dusted dreams in a grand parade,
Life's fun conundrums are here to be played.

So gather your friends, let's bake up a storm,
In this whimsical world, we're all in warm.
With laughter as icing, we'll share each tale,
In the riddles of cake, we shall prevail.

The Enchanted Oven

In a kitchen where secrets dwell,
An oven's hum casts a spell.
Flour flies like dreams in flight,
Whisking chaos, what a sight!

The timer ticks with a playful grin,
Flavors dance, let the fun begin.
Sugar sprinkles in the air,
Baking's magic everywhere!

Cakes and pies with laughter bloom,
Each one fills a tiny room.
Frosting swirls like wild delight,
In every bite, a joke takes flight!

So take a slice, let worries part,
In this oven, you'll find your heart.
With each layer, the truth unwinds,
Sweet surprises the soul finds!

A Dash of Intrigue

A sprinkle of spice, what could it mean?
A recipe lost, or a playful scene?
Cinnamon whispers, nutmeg schemes,
In this kitchen, nothing's as it seems!

The chocolate melts with a sly little wink,
While icing rolls in, it's more than you think.
A dash of salt, a pinch of glee,
A cake unfolds its mystery!

Beneath the frosting, a riddle stirs,
With cherry filling and chocolate blurs.
Each slice offers clues, they're hidden well,
What puzzles await? Only time will tell!

So grab a fork, dig in with flair,
Solve the puzzle layered with care.
For in this treat, you'll surely see,
The fun of baking is the key!

The Marzipan Mystery

Marzipan figures in colorful rows,
Tiny delights with secrets to pose.
A unicorn here, a dragon there,
These edible wonders are beyond compare!

With almond dreams and sugar dust,
Each shape holds a ticklish trust.
What stories lie beyond their glaze?
In each sugary figure, a merry phase!

A twist of fate, a flavorful guise,
A cake like this, it always surprises.
With every bite, the laughter grows,
For in this joy, the heart bestows!

So take a morsel, take a chance,
In marzipan's dance, join the prance.
Sweet enigmas await your taste,
In this sugary world, make haste!

Sweet Labyrinths

In winding paths of cake and cream,
Sweet labyrinths weave a playful dream.
Chocolate rivers, frosting hills,
In this maze, delight fulfills!

With every corner, a flavor awaits,
Caramel swirls and berry plates.
The map's in crumbs, just take a bite,
Navigate this treat with pure delight!

A cherry doorway, a lemon gate,
Curious paths, oh, don't be late!
Each slice you take leads to new cheer,
In this sweet world, there's nothing to fear!

So venture forth, with fork in hand,
In the puzzle of cakes, feel the grand.
For in these layers, let joy unfurl,
And savor the sweetness that life can swirl!

A Slice of Uncertainty

When you open the box, what will you find?
Surprises layer sweet, but not well aligned.
Maybe a cherry, or maybe just cream,
Every bite taken, a puzzling dream.

Frosting is thick, hiding secrets untold,
Sprinkles of fortune, like thieves very bold.
Is it a birthday or just a plain snack?
The flavors are swirling, there's no turning back.

Each forkful a question, a moment to taste,
Like a jigsaw of joy, never goes to waste.
Sugar and laughter blend into delight,
Who knew that a dessert could take flight?

With layers of humor, we slice through the mess,
Every nibble a giggle, no need to impress.
In a world full of crumbs, let's savor the play,
Because life's most funny in a sugary way.

Crumbs of Curiosity

A cookie's crumbled fate, what will it be?
Chocolate chunks whisper secrets, oh me!
Baking brings wonder, through oven's warm glow,
Each batch a new riddle, what answers will show?

Sprinkles that scatter like wild little thoughts,
Cookie dough dreams in the warmth, it begot.
With every new flavor, a journey we roam,
How sweet are the questions that lead us back home.

The milk's in a glass, it dances with fun,
Together they mingle, a duo well done.
What's a pie without laughter, a tart without cheer?
Every morsel we munch draws us ever near.

So grab a fork, friend, let's dig into fate,
Delights hold the keys, but give us a plate.
With crumbs of curiosity, we'll laugh and we'll savor,
This riddle's a feast, and joy's our behavior.

Whipped Whispers of Fate

In a bowl, dreams mix with a wisp of delight,
Whipped cream's soft laughter takes flight in the night.
Each dollop a hopeful little joke in the air,
Whispers of fate dance like ribbons everywhere.

Filling the heart like a cake layered high,
With wit and with whim, we'll soar toward the sky.
Baking confessions wrapped tight in a bite,
A sweetened enigma, oh what a sight!

Sprinkle on giggles, then drizzle with glee,
Pie crusts tell stories, just wait and you'll see.
Turntables of fortune, they spin and they twirl,
While frosting's a canvas for dreams to unfurl.

So gather your friends and let troubles just fade,
In this bakery riddle, no mistakes are made.
With whipped whispers of fate, we'll follow the theme,
Because laughter's the secret infused in the cream.

The Curious Recipe of Being

To live among spices, oh what a delight,
A pinch of adventures, a dash of insight.
Measure your joy in the sweetest of ways,
Baking new moments, a dance that displays.

Sift through your worries, like flour through hands,
Whisking up dreams in immeasurable brands.
Heat up your passions, let them bubble and swell,
In this curious mixture, there's magic to tell.

Layer your stories like cakes in a stack,
Favors can mingle, none ever go slack.
A taste of the past, with hope on the rise,
Every slice tells a story, a fresh surprise.

So grab your spatula, let's make a new plan,
In this recipe of being, we're all part of the pan.
With humor and sweetness, our hearts intertwine,
Each ingredient's awkward, yet splendidly fine.

Tiers of Existence

In layers stacked, the truth reside,
With sprinkles bright, they cannot hide.
Each slice reveals a different tale,
With whipped cream on a paper sail.

The candle's flame flickers with glee,
As forks and laughter dance with me.
A cherry on top, a puzzling delight,
In each hearty bite, the world feels right.

Whisking through problems, like batter so sweet,
With every dilemma, we savor the treat.
A recipe of joy that we all can share,
With frosting of pranks floating through the air.

So grab your fork, let chaos unfold,
With humor and sweetness, this life is gold.
For when we confuse, we learn and we play,
In the kitchen of quirks, we're never away.

The Icing on the Enigma

A puzzle adorned, with flavors galore,
Like hidden gems behind a door.
The icing drips, a mystery neat,
Each bite unwinds a tasty feat.

With frosting swirls that twist and twine,
I giggle hard at riddles divine.
Questions like sprinkles, scattered they fall,
The cake of confusion, a party for all.

Candles flicker with playful intent,
Wrapping our woes in sweet merriment.
Laughter bursts forth like soda pop,
In a riddle where fun is the cream on top.

We serve up smiles on a whimsical plate,
Chasing the shadows of questions we state.
With forks at the ready, let's dig in the fun,
For riddles and icing have only begun.

Sweet Questions

What flavor's the sky when dawn breaks wide?
Is it chocolate dreams or vanilla tide?
Each question a slice on a platter so bright,
Dancing with joy, in the warm morning light.

Layered in laughs, the answers may shock,
With fruits of wisdom tucked inside each block.
As cream whirls around, we savor the quest,
In this circus of flavors, we find our best.

Are mysteries sweet, a taste on the tongue?
Or simply a song that we've yet to hum?
With each little bite, a chuckle will rise,
In the banquet of riddles, we feast with surprise.

So come take a slice, let's unravel the fun,
With sugar-coated thoughts, our journey's begun.
Questions like frosting, we'll whip up a spree,
For every bright answer is sweet jubilee.

Cakewalk Through Conundrums

Tiptoe through puzzles, just like a cake,
With each little challenge, our minds start to wake.
A hop, skip, and jump, with sprinkles in hand,
Our laughter a melody, sweet and unplanned.

A puzzling pie chart of frosting delight,
Each question a candle, glowing so bright.
Let's slice through confusion, share in the cheer,
For each crumb of wisdom, we hold very dear.

Balancing flavors, a delightful dance,
In this cakewalk of riddles, we take our chance.
From fruity dilemmas to chocolatey dreams,
Life's baked with fun, or so it seems.

So gather around, let's celebrate more,
With laughter and cake, who could ask for more?
In this sweet parade, we'll skip with delight,
For a conundrum's just frosting, making things bright!

www.ingramcontent.com/pod-product-compliance
Lightning Source LLC
Chambersburg PA
CBHW051655160426
43209CB00004B/912